SUPPLY-SIDE REFRIED:
The Trump/Republican Scam To Rob Americans Blind, Again!

By

Jim Green

DEDICATED TO: [The Unvarnished Truth]....

The Republican agenda, today, is to lie, cheat, and rob to get elected—so they can lie, cheat and rob the American people blind, once elected!

ISBN-13:
978-1542863438

ISBN-10:
1542863430

PROLOGUE

Hang on folks, WE are about to get "Supply-Side Refried"….. Trump/the Republicans in Congress are preparing to shaft the American people, again!

First, they start the fraud that the Koch brothers [hereafter KB--a metaphor, and fact, for the 1%] needs more money [in the face of the greatest wealth disparity in American history!]—and they want to stuff the pockets of the KB's with a whole bunch of cash [including Trump?]—and send the bill to our grandchildren!

And the most offensive part of this fraud is the bald-faced lie that they are doing it for US—because history has shown that it causes unemployment! It's a crock, folks—and we need to SPEAK UP! Ref: WHY DID WE LET FLINT ROT INTO DECAY: And Usher In A Trump Presidency?, Amazon/Kindle

The Supply-Side scam—started by the Reagan administration in 1980, has a shelf-life of about 7 years before the economy collapses under the weight of this evil scam—[to rob America blind]--sending the economy into meltdown, to wit:

As it did on October 19, 1987—when the Stock Market lost a quarter of its value on that day—the largest one day decline since the Great Depression;

And, the Stock Market crash in the Fall of 2008--on September 29, 2008—with a 777 point loss on that day--the loss of 700,000 jobs a month—and resulting in a staggering 10% unemployment [hereafter UE] rate for most of the next year!

And in both instances, Congress tagged the American people to pay the bill for this corrupt Republican mismanagement or our economy—[i.e., the Republican's pandering to PURE GREED—and to pay for their seat in Congress]….. and driving up massive deficits for our grandchildren to pay!

Because folks, the only way to put a floor under these meltdowns—to stop the hemorrhaging—*IS TO BUY OUR WAY OUT!*

And the irony, when Baker was the Secretary of the Treasury under Reagan—and he drove up the deficit to save the economy in 1987—it didn't even raise an eyebrow in the press….but when President Obama was given that grim—but essential---[total meltdown of the economy was the alternative]—the Tea Party reminded us daily that President Obama, is black.......

The Trump/Republican agenda to pull the Supply-Side scam on the American people—is only on the drawing board at this point.....but they have made crystal-clear every intention to carry out this crime against the American people.....with Paul Ryan in the House their thief-in-charge....!

And how they can keep a straight face—and tell their *BALD-FACE LIES* to the American people—escapes me—calling them "psychopaths" just isn't a big enough word!

Apologize for so many exclamation marks, folks, but I see much of the Republican agenda, almost since Lincoln—much of the 20th Century, has been about what is wrong....harmful....like GREED, racism\hate—in America—not what is right.....and I just have to express my outrage....Why anyone would vote Republican, today, escapes me....and I believe one of my most accurate books, given the current Republican agenda is: IT IS IMPOSSIBLE TO BE A CHRISTIAN, AND VOTE REPUBLICAN, Amazon/Kindle

With rare exception....show me a Republican in Congress, today, and I'll show you an *INSUFFERABLE JERK*---Like Cotton from Arkansas....what a CREEP.....and bottom-feeder....still pandering to his racist faction and scum who wants to relegate America to the 8th Century, BC--

-and what does this tell us about the folk who voted to put them there…..? For example….so far Trump is obsessed with shadow boxing with imaginary enemies….and America is being dragged along on Trump's agenda to pander to "our frightened ones"—and ISIS prayers are being answered by this madness…..Sad! Sad for Americans, and America!

To reverse engineer what you are about to hear in the next few weeks….in the Republican's perpetrating this crime on the American people---could be months, may be days….

But they will decry the taxes paid by the KB/our corporations is way too high……and they must be lowered….[and the most devious part of this BS is that they will say they are doing it for us….the American people—and not to pander to the GREED of the KB----SURE!

The BS theory behind this is that these taxes prevent the KB from building factories all across our fair land….where jobs will rain down like moonbeams—and we will all live happily ever after—*IT IS PURE BS…..A FAIRY TALE…..*

And what they did under Reagan/Bush is consummate proof: The KB stuffed the windfall of cash in their pocket, built factories in Sri Lanka, and fraudulently hid their profits in the Cayman Islands—to defraud investing in America! And their CRIME created the greatest wealth disparity in American history!

There is another wrinkle in here…..the smart Republicans know the truth…..but some are so myopic—we can't be sure…..and chalking up to stupidity may be too harsh—let's just call them the *TRUE BELIEVERS*….

That is, those who actually believe the most pernicious fraud every perpetrated on the American people since WW II—that "The market can provide anybody wanting a job, with a job"….IT IS PURE BS!

And what makes it so difficult in pointing out the fallacy in this statement is that millions of Americans….including Democrats in Congress….have been indoctrinated with the propaganda….since youth, that this is true….it is like a belief in Santa Claus….until we realize it isn't true…..and it sounds logical….until we look at the data……

And, all of our Job Creation since WW II has been based on this false belief….i.e., if when lieve we have the solution to a problem….we are not looking elsewhere for the solution….and that is the dynamic, here….

But look up the data and you will find—with this as the sole policy driving our Job Creation since WW II—that this has not resulted in a UE rate above 3%, since 1953! Leaving millions jobless in its wake, and creating an epidemic of gun violence in America!

And another part of the Republican lie is that if we go along with these massive tax cuts for the KB….they will create jobs with the windfall of cash….and as noted above—*THAT IS PURE BS!*

And the loss in income to the Market is compounded exponentially with each percentage point of increase in unemployment, above 3% [See: D/UE LAW, elsewhere]…...

A few closing comments in the Prologue…..Oscar Wilde averred "The only truly worthless opinion is an unbiased one"—so bias, agreed—but always in the interest in getting at the larger goal—the truth….

Incidentally, I published my first book on my 78th birthday [I am currently 82]—and not that I write that fast, or well—the materials were all there for the better part of the past 30 years, give or take, gathering dust—it was just a matter of pulling them together in some order—also, don't believe any book should be over 60 pages, plus/minus— i.e., can be read in the crapper--two hours, max--lol—but it seems best summed up by a very astute observer [wish I could recall their name to give credit]: Persons who write do so because they have no choice [it is a compulsion, an addiction..]—they become an "author", however, when people start reading what they have written….

Finally, a note to the reader—my system is a little unorthodox—but my objective always is to communicate with the reader…if I accurately convey my point….whether you agree, or disagree….maybe vehemently disagree—objective met….decorum less important…and the printed page is sometimes right on the nose….others, look like a kidnap for ransom note….so please just look for content…..and the papers and letters are not in sequence, and apologize for redundancy [please look for the nuggets…Thx--lol]—also, if you are a "typo-wonk"—are more concerned with sentence structure, etc., than content—you probably won't like my writing—and you will find a wayward capital letter, here and there, and appearing out of place and used for emphasis—or a missing page…Hey, I'm an Indie….I chalk most up to editorial license and tongue-in-cheek [except when I am dead serious], self-effacing humor—so apologies, here—[I seriously support: Take what you do seriously, but never yourself….]….

Just look for content, please….THX

CHAPTER ONE

The following email, in the Congressional Record, from Newsmax, is being brought front and center because it underscores that SUPPLY-SIDE REFRIED is a SCAM [without ANY justification] by Trump/Republicans to STEAL from the American people...to pander to KB GREED, and as payback for donations......while sending the bill to pay for their tax cuts for the wealthy to our grandchildren to pay!

"Millionaires Tell Congress: Raise Our Taxes"

"A well-heeled group calling itself the Patriotic Millionaires for Fiscal Strength is planning to lobby Capitol Hill on Wednesday with an unusual request: "Tax me."

" With the supercommittee's Thanksgiving-eve deadline less than two weeks away, members of Patriotic Millionaires — open only to people with incomes of $1 million and higher — plan to testify at a hearing on jobs and taxes, then meet with supercommittee members and their staffs, other Congressional leaders and lawmakers from the Tea Party Caucus.

"It will take all patriotic Americans working together to fix the problems irresponsible politicians caused by cutting taxes for millionaires at the same time they put two wars on the nation's credit card," insists Erica Payne of Patriotic Millionaires. "We need to pay for the choices we make. These Patriotic Millionaires are willing to do that. On Wednesday, we will ask our elected officials if they are willing to do the same."

"They are willing to pay more in taxes because the sacrifice is both an ethical and patriotic decision," according to a group statement. "It is made in the hopes of allowing the United States to continue to be a leader economically, politically, and morally. Any deal reached by the supercommittee that does not ask millionaires to pay their fair share should be vetoed."

"Initially formed to urge President Barack Obama to let the Bush-era tax cuts expire for people making more than $1 million a year, membership has now swelled to 200, and includes more than a dozen current and former Google employees; actress Edie Falco ("The Sopranos"); the founders of Esprit, the Princeton Review, and Ask.com; philanthropist Michael Steinhardt; economist Nouriel Roubini; financial guru Andrew Tobias; top executives from Warburg, Pincus; and filmmaker Abigail Disney.

"An outpouring of public support encouraged them to continue their fight," the group says, citing the following:

- Only 375,000 Americans have incomes of over $1 million.
- Between 1979 and 2007, incomes for the wealthiest 1 percent of Americans rose by 281 percent.

- During the Great Depression, millionaires had a top marginal tax rate of 68 percent.
- In 1963 millionaires had a top marginal tax rate of 91 percent.
- In 1976 millionaires had a top marginal tax rate of 70 percent.
- Today, millionaires have a top marginal tax rate of 35 percent.
- Reducing the income tax on top earners is one of the most inefficient ways to grow the economy, according to the Congressional Budget Office.
- 44 percent of Congress people are millionaires.

The Bush tax cuts were never meant to be permanent, and letting them expire for the top 2 percent would pay down the debt by $700 billion over the next 10 years."

CHAPTER TWO

President Obama/Council of Economic Advisers:

The Democrats lost the election because they DIDN'T FIX UNEMPLOYMENT! It is the reason over 70% of Americans believe "We are moving in the wrong direction"!

But the reason is not from lack of interest, or dedication, on the part of us Democrats—[or even prevented by an obstructionist Republican Congress]--- RATHER, it is because we Democrats drank the Kool Aid that "The market can provide anybody wanting a job, with a job".....and we passed The HIRE Act--HR 2847—in 2009 as our Job Creation law—but it is an "out to lunch" law—because it is a "stop-gap" law waiting for the market to solve the problem [as opposed to "renewal funding"]—

And we Democrats then stood on one foot and then the other waiting on the Market to do something IT IS IMPOSSIBLE FOR THE MARKET TO DO [the issue isn't ideological—it regards something THAT DOESN'T WORK]!

But we Democrats went on BELIEVING in spite of the data that this, our method of Job Creation since WW II--has NOT resulted in a jobless rate below 3% since 1953! Leaving millions jobless in its wake, created our inner-cities with 60% minority unemployment, drug economies, and an epidemic of gun violence!

But wishing hope against hope that something will work--THAT DOESN'T WORK—is not limited to us Democrats—and is akin to those folk in the Rust Belt who believe Trump's promise that he will create "millions of jobs"………..

UNLESS, Trump can wrap his brain around the fact that Hunphrey-Hawkins [currently HR 1000] is a PRO-MARKET solution…and given "automation", alone, is INDISPENSABLE to the EFFECTIVE functioning of our 21st Century market economy! AND, that Trump recognizes that unemployment adversely impacts the "bottom line"—i.e., that people do not buy what we manufacture, when they are jobless [which inexplicably is not cited by Democrats that we need to change the dialogue], to wit:

OUR SLUGGISH ECONOMY RESULTNG FROM THE LAW OF DIMINISHED INCOME TO THE MARKET FROM UNEMPLOYMENT [hereafter D/UE LAW]

Short Definition:

3% is the zero-sum threshold above which unemployment starts substantially undermining the Market--and the loss in income to the Market is compounded exponentially with each percentage point of increase in unemployment, above 3%..

The Solution: HR 1000 [in Committee], THE NEIGHBOR-TO-NEIGHBOR JOB CREATION ACT

[NTN]Amazon: a Pro-Market, deficit-neutral federally mandated Social Insurance, owned by our employed—to provide a fund to hire-train our unemployed. Jobs beget jobs, and this will create more "private-sector" jobs in 6 mos, than HR 2847, in six years!

Jim Green, Democrat candidate for Congress, 2000

Thank you for contacting the White House!

CHAPTER THREE

President Obama/Presidential Innovation Fellows:

Since WW II our single method of Job Creation in America has been based on the belief/propaganda that "The market can provide anybody wanting a job, with a job"……

And when it didn't work--we pretended it did, and drifted into Santa Clause-like wishful thinking—asserting "it is the American way", or "God's will"—or some such lie we told ourselves--as rational Job Creation, in a changing world, drifted further and further away…..

For instance, this method of Job Creation has not resulted in a UE rate below 3% since 1953, but we limped along—terrorized by McCarthyism, and leaving millions jobless—and by the mid-1970's the colliding forces of globalization, automation, technology reached critical mass, resulting in a cosmic shift in the world economy—with subsequent "High and persistent unemployment pervasive throughout the OECD since the mid-1970's", according to Dr. William F. Mitchell, and every credible economist.

And, going forward the data got even more grim—i.e., since 1980 we have had excessive UE 70% of the time [twice that of preceding years], and by the Crash of 2008—8 million were rendered jobless—[and in spite of an extremely anemic recovery we inched down from

10% to 5% UE, inexplicably still relying on the above method]—--

And with the result that by the September 2016 DOL Jobs Report, we still have 8 million Americans looking for work, that can't find any…..and in an economy limping along on a flat tire—as a direct result of high UE, and a Republican Congress determined to sabotage America—for political reasons--

The lesson is: Our choices are adapt and change in a world that is changing—whether we like it or not—or be forced to create a Police State to hold in place antiquated and unworkable laws and policies [in this case re our Job Creation]—and sadly, America has opted for the latter—and we need look no further than the police marching in lock-step in Charlotte, this past week, as proof!

The flaw in all of this is based on simple common sense: "The mechanic can't fix the engine without the proper tools"—and when Jobs, Jobs, Jobs is the major mantra in this election—fixing unemployment is hopeless so long as we insist on a method of Job Creation—THAT DOESN'T WORK!

Proposed Solutions: HR 1000, and FULL EMPLOYMENT IS A PRO-MARKET CONCEPT, Amazon

Jim Green, Democrat opponent to Lamar Smith, 2000

Thank you for contacting the White House!

CHAPTER FOUR

Editor: NY TIMES

Capitalism is ideal in producing and selling corn flakes and cars—It doesn't work in solving "social problems" such as unemployment and our healthcare....

And when we have tried "privatization" to solve our social problems—it has been a disaster:

Specifically, essential programs have been cut—such as the elimination of text books from the Job Corps education program—to increase profits, and cronyism has run rampant—

And in our "for profit" healthcare system, billions of dollars are siphoned away from the premiums we send in—and do not go to the healthcare of ANYONE—but rather is used to pay for lobbyists, to make the CEO's filthy rich—and spent on propaganda ads to keep it that way!

Additionally, President Obama had a weapon in 2009, not available to FDR: Were it not for the $800 billion in Social Security Insurance moneys percolating up through our economy annually, ie., in 2008—we would not be talking about having narrowly averted another Great Depression—We would be buried in one!

The truth is, we have a blended economic system—and the two components are, in fact, indispensable to each other:

Social Insurance is a vital ingredient in building a vibrant and decent society—And, invent a better widget, sell the company for a million bucks, and retire in Florida [capitalism]—is as well a vital ingredient in building a vibrant and decent society.

So why do we have this war of words pitting the two against each other—rather than educating the American people regarding the indispensable symbiotic relationship they have to each other?

Were it not for the $2 trillion + Washington infuses back into the economy annually—capitalism would fold in a NY Second!

And yet, most Republicans ask God in their prayers at night to be protected from communists, or socialists, or even worse "liberals"—[i.e., monsters under their bed] with "liberal" henceforth to be replaced with the word "Christian"…..

Regarding "unemployment" [hereafter UE]—it is essential that we evolve, and given "automation", alone, in our 21st Century economy we need to look upon UE the same as we look upon Cancer, Polio, or AIDS, as a ubiquious disease—a menace to society, in need of eradication….via [15 USC § 3101]—which would restrict our UE to 3%, permanently!

Best regards,

Jim Green

CHAPTER FIVE

President Obama:

It is impossible to reform our broken criminal justice system—absent our creating a viable job creation program in America.

And while it is generally believed that we do have a job creation program, in fact, we do not!

We have the BELIEF that "the market can provide anybody wanting a job, with a job"—but the data shows that only ONCE since WW II has minority unemployment in our inner-cities, with drug economies, and an epidemic of homicides [i.e., not fixing unemployment has turned our inner-cities into war zones, and created a breeding ground for our inexplicable incarceration rate].

Further this "belief" has been a stumbling block in finding a solution for our pervasive unemployment--In short, we have not been looking for a solution—because our policy makers believe we have one—and apparently few have looked at the data....

Also, ignored in the discussion this belief resulted in an unemployment rate below 3%--in 1953—leaving millions jobless in its wake-- and has resulted in:

60% is that unemployment is a "social" problem, with adverse, and oft severe social consequences—both for the individual, as well as the larger society [i.e., it is the responsibility of the larger society to solve]—

With tentacles integral to all of the social problems facing Americans, today—for instance, ending unemployment is integral to Criminal Justice Reform, and the repair of our crumbling infrastructure....

Further, in 1975 we spent $5 educating our youth, for every $1 we spent on prisons.....by the mid-1990's [with the American people having been terrorized by the Willie Horton ad—and on an hysterical prison building spree] our competing tax dollars tipped in favor of prisons—and at present we spend more on prisons, than on educating our youth.

The irony in all of this is that we have the "legal authorization", on the books to reduce our unemployment rate to 3%, tomorrow [15 USC § 3101—and deficit-neutral HR 1000, currently in Committee]—and also ignored in this context, is that President Obama had a weapon in addressing our economic meltdown in 2008, not available to FDR— and that is the $800 billion in Social Security Insurance claims percolating up through our economy—and in the absence of which--We would be buried in another Great Depression!

Turning the page—and given "automation", alone, is critical going forward in the 21st Century—and is a "win-win"—the American people win, and the market wins....

Ref: FULL EMPLOYMENT IS A PRO-MARKET CONCEPT, Amazon

Jim Green, Democrat opponent to Lamar Smith, 2000

CHAPTER SIX

President Obama/Council of Economic Advisers:

Our network of market-driven economies [the OECD, including the U.S]—currently have a pernicious job creation modality—with resulting high and pervasive unemployment since the mid-1970's—and on a collision course with the future—i.e., given "automation", alone, fewer and fewer jobs are being created with each passing year, as we advance into the 21st Century....

This job creation modality is based on the erroneous propaganda/belief that "the market can provide anybody wanting a job, with a job"—and yet, only ONCE since WW II has this modality resulted in an unemployment rate below 3%--in 1953—leaving millions jobless in its wake, and has resulted in our inner-cities turning into war zones--with 60% minority unemployment, drug economies, and an epidemic of homicides.

The irony in this disaster, however, is that the U.S. correctly anticipated this result in 1978—and provided the American people with a solution, i.e., the "legal authorization" [15 USC § 3101] to limit our unemployment henceforth to "3%", and as we advance into the 21st Century—

With a ton of cash poured into our political system, and a mind-set with both feet planted on the plantation—-- special interests sabotaged this law to prevent its implementation—to the detriment of Americans, and America [ISIS is the least of our worries in America, when we have the Republican party]!

Unemployment is a "social" problem, with adverse social consequences....it is solely the province of the larger society to solve—and leaving the solution to anything as erratic as the market—as we do now—is patently absurd!

The bottom line is that unemployment is a NO ONE WINS....the jobless lose, civility loses, and the market loses, to wit:

THE LAW OF DIMINISHED INCOME TO THE MARKET FROM UNEMPLOYMENT [hereafter D/UE LAW]

3% is the zero-sum threshold above which unemployment triggers inflation by diminishing labor training and skills, under-utilizing capital resources, reducing the rate of productivity advance, increasing unit labor costs, reducing the general supply of goods and services--and the loss in income to the Market is compounded exponentially with each percentage point of increase in unemployment, above 3%.

Ref: HR 1000 [in Committee], and FULL EMPLOYMENT IS A PRO-MARKET SOLUTION, Amazon

Jim Green, Democrat opponent to Lamar Smith, 2000

Thank You!

Thank you for contacting the White House

CHPATER SEVEN

THE HISTORY OF HOW WE GOT WHERE WE ARE
[WW II to Present]

Following WW II, President Truman signed into law the [FULL] EMPLOYMENT ACT of 1946, to provide employment for our returning troops.

Ironically, half-way around the world, Australia codified into their law an almost identical Bill, and for the same reason—

Difference is—Australia actually put their law into effect, and over the next 30 years it was intrinsic to employment policy in Australia that "anybody wanting to work should be able to find a job"—and save for a brief recession in 1961/62 their unemployment was 2%, or less. This period is still referred to as their "Golden Age", in Australia.

Unforeseen by either country, however, in the mid-1970's the world economy underwent a major paradigm shift as a result of the colliding forces of automation, globalization, technology, etc., reaching a critical mass—in brief, an adjustment towards modernity—From a perverse perspective, we became victims of our success....

The instability caused by this transition, however, resulted in a malaise, and ushered in the ill-winds of greed-driven neo-liberalism with its indifference to unemployment, and the likes of Thatcher and Reagan—and the menace of this greed-driven agenda was exploded by Bush II, resulting in obscene disparities in wealth that persists, and is the cause of much friction between right and left, to this day.

It also ushered in high and pervasive unemployment throughout our market-driven economies, the OECD—with 6% unemployment in Australia now the norm, and double-digit unemployment common throughout the Eurozone, to this day.

As a result of the "malaise", however, the U.S. took an aggressive, pro-active role in addressing the, above, economic shift—and in 1978 President Carter signed into law one of the most important laws in the 20th Century--an expansion of President Truman's full employment, i.e., Pro-Market 15 USC § 3101--which provides a "*legal authorization*" to create a "reservoir of public employees" [*indispensable to the effective functioning of a 21st Century market economy*]--at any time our unemployment in America exceeds "3%"—

But in spite of 3% unemployment being the threshold point above which unemployment starts substantially undermining the Market—this *legal authorization* has never been implemented--

And in spite of deficit-neutral HR 1000, or The Neighbor-To-Neighbor Job Creation Act—A federally mandated Social Insurance, owned by our employed, to provide a fund to hire/train our unemployed—[more on the critical need to apply this job creation methodology in a 21st Century market economy, ahead]....

Ref: FULL EMPLOYMENT IS A PRO-MARKET CONCEPT, Amazon/Kindle

Jim Green, Democrat opponent to Lamar Smith, Congress, 2000

CHAPTER EIGHT
THE HISTORY OF HOW WE GOT WHERE WE ARE
[Mid-1970's to Present]

In the mid-1970's, the colliding forces of automation, technology, globalization, etc., reached a critical mass—resulting in a Market no longer capable of producing the jobs necessary to its viability, and causing ubiquitous unemployment in all of the OECD countries—and leaving their leaders conflicted, ever since, regarding the displaced employee. Eurozone unemployment is still in double digits, and Greece and Spain both in excess of 20%, plus. High unemployment was also a major factor in Arab Spring.

In the U.S., we took a pro-active role in addressing this economic shift—and in 1978 President Carter signed into law 15 USC § 3101--which "authorizes" the creation of a "reservoir of public employment" at any time our unemployment in America exceeds "3%".

In 1979, however, and in a panic over Humphrey-Hawkins—our ultra-conservative foundations, and desperate to promote the Supply-Side fraud, embraced a flawed paper by an obscure MIT student, David L. Birch "The Job Generation Process"; and [with lots of cash] gave his paper biblical importance, and every president since has cited his finding as gospel.

Birch's paper concluded that "small businesses" were the greatest generator of new jobs—problem is, for the purposes of policy-making—it is BS. In a study at Harvard University in 2010, "The Myth of Small Business Job Creation" The research shows "no systematic relationship between firm size and growth." And that small businesses can actually detract from job growth.

In spite of this, however, Washington struggles, still, to make this antiquated notion, work--that it is only the market that can create jobs—and the result has been a disaster, politically as well as otherwise!

It would be impossible to still have 7.8% unemployment—if we were on the right path—and among other problems with this concept--if the market fails, the unemployed are out of luck.

Further, unemployment is a "social" problem we are seeking to address with a highly unstable, incompatible entity: The Market

What apparently isn't clear going forward is that an expanding and contracting public workforce is an *indispensable* component to the *effective* functioning of a modern market economy—

The market thrives when we have a robust, employed, consuming workforce—and overlooked is that HR 1000 [currently in Committee], and the proposed "Neighbor-To-Neighbor Job Creation Act" www.Inclusivism.org [both authorized under Humphrey-Hawkins], are deficit-neutral--Pro-Market "win-win" solutions:

The American people win, and capitalism wins—

Jim Green, Democrat candidate for Congress, 2000

CHAPTER NINE

Friends: In the event you have gotten this far—according to the Federal Election Commission, I am a candidate for president in the 2016 election—and rest assured I am not delusional, or like Trump…on an ego trip…..I filed solely to deliver a message—you are reading it—and to urge passage of the above legislation….

To Whom It May Concern—in Washingon:

OUR CHOICES ARE: Adapt and change in a world that is changing, whether we like it or not, OR be forced to create a Police State to hold our anachronistic policies, practices and laws in place—

And in America, today, we have chosen the latter…..and as only one pernicious example, of thousands—Ferguson is the result….

In a comedic, but religious context we hear of persons asking God for a sign—anything—which will warn us that we are on the wrong path, and need to change direction…..and our Police State choice, above, is *our sign*…..few are listening….

To illustrate a critical area in which we need to adapt and change in a 21st Century economy: We have far more work that needs to be done in America, than we have persons to fill these jobs—And 86% of Americans believe that "Anybody wanting to work should be able to find a job"---So, why on earth *in a democracy*, do we have 9 million jobless Americans—[per the 11/14 DOL Jobs report]?

The answer is because our *method* of job creation in America is based on a Fairy Tale! Specifically, our current *one and only* job creation methodology in America, is based on the myth/sacred cow:

"The market can provide anybody wanting a job, with a job"—

Problem is—it is pure BS—and only *once* since WW II has this methodology resulted in an unemployment rate below 3%--in 1953 [i.e., which translates into 5 million left jobless]--because the market *cannot* create enough jobs—in short, the jobs for this 5 million jobless--*don't exist*!

The right-wing propaganda mills trick our fools into believing that the market has created this 5 million jobs, but because those on welfare are "lazy and don't want to work" this 5 million jobs go unfilled—but that is *pure balderdash!*

The vast majority of persons on welfare, are there *because* the *market* cannot create enough jobs, i.e., the market lacks the viability to create these jobs—the jobs simply *do not exist*!

And as further proof, according to the CBO, on our current path it will be 2017 before America returns to even an anemic 5.5% unemployment rate [following the Great Recession] and if the market fails in the interim—the jobless are out of luck!

Further, this travesty is compounded because the Republicans cling to devious and discredited Supply Side Economics [to this day] as a solution, to wit:

Siphon America's wealth away from the consuming middle—give this windfall of cash to the Koch Bros [a metaphor for the 1%, hereafter "KB"]—they will build factories all across our fair land—everyone will have a job in the corporation—and we will all live happily ever after—Yes, folks it is a fairy tale!

And what we learned from this dark cloud over America is what Bush I called it long ago—before America was subjected to this devious scam—i.e., Supply-Side is "VooDoo Economics"!

So why have we allowed ourselves to be deceived by this Republican scam—[handcrafted by a plutocracy/oligarchy that still has one foot on the plantation]? But I don't want to giveaway the surprise ending—and some of my response isn't printable….! Further, and to say it up front….I am a capitalist—I support 100%: Build a better widget, sell it for a million bucks, and retire in South Florida….it is the Republican agenda, today, that is anti-market…more on this throughout…..

When President Carter handed the reigns over to Reagan in 1981—he left America with a very modest

$60 billion deficit—as a direct result of Supply-Side, however, when Republicans held the White House [Clinton actually cut the deficit]—this $60 billion ballooned to a staggering $10 trillion by 2008—and it has cost Americans an additional $7+trillion to clean up this Republican mess—

Ask any economist: Our only way out of a meltdown *is to buy our way out!* [it was the lesson learned from the Great Depression].

And anyone who thinks McCain, had he been elected, would not have addressed this with a Stimulus, the same as President Obama in 2009—is stuffed between the ears with rice pudding……

Further, we learned that we cannot siphon America's wealth away from the consuming middle, and give it to the "KB"—without sending our economy into meltdown—as occurred in 1987 and 2008—in short, the Supply-Side scam has a shelf-life of about 7 years before the economy collapses—and as noted, costing the taxpayers trillions to put a floor under a disappearing economy!

And another fallout/direct result from this dark chapter is the disparity in wealth it has created in America—AKA the "wealth gap"--and currently the "richest 1 percent in the United States now own more wealth than the bottom 90 percent"—the second highest in our history, the first was just before the Great Depression.

A couple of other factors that played into the above scenario—when every waking moment in capitalism is spent pondering how to eliminate as many of us humans, as possible, from the workplace—to increase "profits"—why, on Earth, would we look to the market to solve our unemployment crisis in America?

As well, few things on earth are more unstable than the market....we can count on one hand the number of corporations in America that were around in 1900....with tens of thousands long since disappeared; and given "automation", alone, the market will produce fewer and fewer jobs the further we advance into the 21st Century.

Further, unemployment is a "social" problem—we, as the larger society have the responsibility to solve—i.e., it is unrealistic to expect the market to solve this problem—the market is in the "for profit" business, not the social work business—and the former would not long be in business--if they were...for example, we should never condemn the CEO for closing a plant when they are losing money—but we should be outraged by a government that doesn't have a clue re the displaced employees.....

Also, unemployment is a _no one wins_ .....the jobless lose, and market loses, to wit:

> 3% is the zero-sum threshold above which unemployment triggers inflation by diminishing labor training and skills, under-utilizing capital resources, reducing the rate of productivity

advance, increasing unit labor costs, and reducing the general supply of goods and services--and the loss in income to the Market is compounded exponentially with each percentage point of increase in unemployment, above 3%.

Short Definition:

3% is the zero-sum threshold above which unemployment starts substantially undermining the Market--and the loss in income to the Market is compounded exponentially with each percentage point of increase in unemployment, above 3%.

In sum, our job creation should be based on: Fix unemployment, and this will fix the market [HR 1000], rather than [our current mind-set] Fix the market, and this in turn fix unemployment [HR 2847] – with a result that has been a disaster—as we inch along in our job recovery, see data above, and when we didn't *Fix Unemployment* a retaliatory electorate ushered in a House filled with lunatics in the 2010 election, and then doubled down in 2014!

Look around—all signs in our economy are up—and yet over two-thirds of our rank and file believe "we are moving in the wrong direction"—their perception is that our economy is in the tank—that we are in an economic malaise—a condition that would disappear overnight if we did, in fact, *Fix Unemployment*!

Best guess is that Congress passed, and President Obama signed into law HR 2847 [the HIRE Act], in 2009—which is based on fix the market, and this will fix unemployment [180 degrees off course]—but they did this because of the pervasive [but false] *belief* that "The market can provide anybody wanting a job, with a job"—it is *pure BS......it doesn't work*! Had we insisted on putting a lawnmower engine in the rocket to get us to the Moon....we would never have gotten there...[same difference]....and all of the empirical evidence is proof HR 2847 didn't create anywhere near the jobs needed...

Jim Green, Democrat opponent to Lamar Smith, Congress, 2000

CHAPTER TEN

HOPPER-READY: THE NEIGHBOR-TO-NEIGHBOR JOB CREATION ACT

[1] PROPOSED LEGISLATION:

THE NEIGHBOR-TO-NEIGHBOR JOB CREATION ACT

A Pro-Market, deficit-neutral, federally mandated, Social Insurance, owned by our employed, to provide a fund to hire/train our unemployed.

SECTION 1. SHORT TITLE.

This Act shall be cited as The Neighbor-To-Neighbor Job Creation Act [To establish employment/training opportunities for the unemployed in compliance with the "Legal Authorization" in Public Law 15 USC § 3101, for the creation of a "reservoir of public employees", anytime our unemployment rate exceeds "3%", with an emphasis on training for market needs, including a training stipend, where there is a shortage of trained workers--hereafter NTN].

SEC. 2. DEFINITIONS.

In this Act the following definitions apply:

(1) SECRETARY- The term `Secretary' means the Secretary of Labor.

(2) STATE- The term `State' has the meaning given such term in section 102(2) of the Housing and Community Development Act (42 U.S.C. 5302(2)).

(3) TRUST FUND- The term `Trust Fund' refers to the Department of Labor Full Employment Trust Fund.

(4) UNIT OF GENERAL LOCAL GOVERNMENT- The term `unit of general local government' has the meaning given such term in section 102(1) of the Housing and Community Development Act (42 U.S.C. 5302(1)).

(5) URBAN COUNTY- The term `urban county' has the meaning given such term in section 102(6) of the Housing and Community Development Act (42 U.S.C. 5302(6)).

(6) WEB SITE- The Secretary shall establish an Internet Web site to serve as an information clearinghouse for job training and employment opportunities funded by the Trust Fund.

SEC. 3. EMPLOYMENT OPPORTUNITY GRANTS TO STATES, LOCAL GOVERNMENT.

(a) Use of Funds-A recipient of a grant under this section shall use the grant primarily for infrastructure repair, including, but not limited to:

(A) The painting and repair of schools, community centers, and libraries.
(B) The restoration and revitalization of abandoned and vacant properties to alleviate blight in distressed and foreclosure-affected areas of a unit of general local government.
(C) The augmentation of staffing in Head Start, child care, and other early childhood education programs to promote school readiness and early literacy.
(D) The renovation and enhancement of maintenance of parks, playgrounds, and other public spaces.

Respectfully Submitted,

Jim Green, Democrat candidate for Congress, Dist 21, TX, 2000

CHAPTER ELEVEN

WHAT WE NEED TO DO GOING FORWARD IN THE 21ST CENTURY:

Inexplicably "public employment" is seen the same as WPA—where millions are employed directly by the federal government—when that model is not only outmoded—it is insufficient to address our problems in the 21st century.

What we need today is an expanding and contracting public workforce—that expands during downturns in the market, and contracts as employees return to the private sector [Google: The Buffer Stock Employment Model]—triggered anytime our unemployment exceeds "3%" [as "authorized" under Humphrey-Hawkins]-- and least understood: This is an INDISPENSABLE component in the effective functioning of our 21st Century Market.

The market thrives when we have a robust, employed, consuming workforce—our manufacturers are sitting on $2 trillion in cash because they do not have consumers for their products—i.e., absent consumers, they lay off employees—[and the Republican solution, Reaganomics, has acted as an accelerate to this downward spiral—and which Romney promises to return us to if he is elected]!

In short, the above model is a "win-win" solution—the American people win, and capitalism wins!

To achieve this, what is being urged is "The Neighbor-To-Neighbor Job Creation Act": A federally mandated, mutual insurance—owned by our employed [from janitor to CEO] to create a fund to hire/train our unemployed.

To be viable, however, our job creation solution _MUST_ contain:

1] Be based on the premise that we have far more work that needs to be done in America, than we have persons to fill these jobs.

2] It MUST have renewable funding.

3] It will not add a dime to our deficit.

To expand briefly, it is currently believed, erroneously, that we need "make work" jobs so that everyone who wants to work will have a job—but this is absurd—and an insult to "Yankee Ingenuity".

We do not have an unemployment crisis from a shortage of jobs, or money—but rather from a shortage of imagination.

Regarding "renewable funding" ALL of our job creation solutions, to date, have been based on the mind-set: "jump start" the market, and the market will in turn create all the jobs we need—and even setting aside that this is untrue, our current job creation is moving at a snail's pace—long past the unemployment benefits drying up—with the CBO projecting that even with the JOBS Act, signed into law on April 6, 2012--it will be 2017 before we return to a barely acceptable 5.5% unemployment rate!

Further, by its nature when we "jump start" --the employment ends when the funding runs out as we learned from the Stimulus—whereas any real fix to our unemployment crisis *demands* renewable funding....

And whether the electorate will accept an unemployment rate hovering around 8% on election day—is the $64,000 question....

Regarding not adding a dime to our deficit—under The Neighbor-To-Neighbor Job Creation Act [NTN], the *funding* to reduce our unemployment to 3% comes from an insurance owned by our employed, rather than added to our deficit—

If one is employed in America, participation in this insurance plan is mandatory—similar in concept to our auto insurance or Social Security Insurance [and without question the most successful social program in American history].

Jobs beget jobs--And with a modest policy cost of 4% of salary we can create more "private-sector" jobs in 6 months, that HR 2847, and the JOBS Act, in 6 years— and unlike these laws—NTN will not add a dime to our deficit!

Finally, this is in total concert with the will of the American people, i.e., that "anybody willing to work should be able to find a job"—and the American people have told our politicians time and again of their willingness to chip in to help their neighbor get a job [and as an *insurance*, as above, it also protects their continued employment]—it is just that Washington is deaf as an adder!

CHAPTER TWELVE

President Obama/Council of Economic Advisers:

Public-Sector jobs strengthen our free-enterprise market economy—i.e., they are a critical component to the viability of our 21st Century economy--rather than weakening the market--as propagandist, with one foot on the plantation, fraudulently deceive the public into believing for the purposes of exploiting American employees.....

Indeed, since WW II, the Koch brothers [both literally, and a metaphor, here, for the 1%] have spent tens of millions buying governors and legislators, to cement "at will" employment in every state [and currently only Montana limits to probationary employees]; and to destroy "collective bargaining", i.e., unions in America—

In sum, they have spent tens of millions of dollars to destroy "employee rights" in America!

To understand the importance of "collective bargaining" for employees, it is informative to take a page from history:

When Hitler became the dictator in Germany, one of his first laws was to make it illegal for more than three persons to gather on the street—and German citizens were subject to immediate arrest if they did.

The same principal is being used by preventing employees putting their heads together, as it were, to bargain for employee rights—and recently one group of employees placed "job security" over a salary increase—with the irony being that the specific objective of "at will" employment—is to destroy "job security"!

In short, the deceptive propaganda to frighten Americans regarding "public-sector" jobs, has but a single parent: To exploit American labor—by some, to assuage deep-seated feelings of inferiority [they can only feel tall, by making others small, in their eyes]---— but most often for just pure GREED!

Where our policies makers go wrong by pandering to some in the oligarchy—and/or buying into this fraudulent propaganda:

Unemployment is a NO ONE WINS—the jobless lose, civility loses, and the market loses, to wit:

THE LAW OF DIMINISHED INCOME TO THE MARKET FROM UNEMPLOYMENT [hereafter D/UE LAW]

Short Definition:

3% is the zero-sum threshold above which unemployment starts substantially undermining the Market--and the loss in income to the Market is compounded exponentially with each percentage point of increase in unemployment, above 3%.

Ref: IT IS IMPOSSIBLE TO BE A CHRISTIAN, AND VOTE REPUBLICAN, Amazon

Jim Green, Democrat opponent to Lamar Smith, 2000

CHAPTER THIRTEEN

FAIL-SAFE ELECTRONIC VOTING

TO THE READER: Given you have gotten this far, and agree with the proposed changes—and particularly given the pernicious Citizens United—our democracy, and the above, or any, progress, will be in peril absent a "fail-safe" electronic voting system. The following is my proposed solution, and like every solution proposed, here, feed-back--your proposed improvement, etc. is welcomed:

THE FAIL-SAFE ELECTRONIC VOTING ACT

1) EVERY electronic voting machine (hereafter EVM), must be inexpensive, identical throughout the U.S. in a 1/150 ratio, and *must count and produce a hard-copy of the recorded votes.* In addition, an extra copy of their recorded votes would be produced (not necessarily a hard-copy), marked "Voter's Copy", and containing "NOTICE: Do Not Destroy Until Every Election On Your Ballot Is Certified". [If Wal-Mart handed us a piece of paper with the words "trust us" as a receipt for our purchases—we would be outraged—and yet, this is our current electronic voting nightmare—but in this case it is our democracy at risk]!

2) *After confirming that their votes are recorded correctly*, the voter would then insert the hard-copy ballot into a software-free (count only) optical scanner (hereafter OS), for a second count. The hard-copy

ballot would be retained by election officials in the event a candidate asks for a recount (*not possible under the current system, and which undermines the legality of each such election*). The EVM and the OS must be manufactured by different companies (which is universally true today).

3) Election officials assigned to oversee the EVM, would be prevented by law from overseeing the OS, and vice-versa, and stiff criminal penalties would be imposed for violations.

4) Further, every EVM would be programmed with raw data re the total registration rolls, by party, and norms for their voting history, etc.,----as an "alert" to a possible irregularity, such as an "under-vote"—or "vote-flipping" etc., and *standards* established to suspend certification where there is an "improbable result", at least temporarily, of a particular election until the discrepancy is cleared up. (This is what computers do best, and it would be very easy to create such a program).

5) At the end of the election day, tallies would be taken from the EVM and the OS, for each candidate. *If the tallies didn't balance for any given election, or if there is an "alert", that election cannot be certified until the "error" is corrected.* If the candidates agree (the victory is certain), minor discrepancies in the count could be disregarded. While probably rare, the Voter, or a random sample of Voters, would be required by law to return their Copy of the recorded votes to the election

office to clear up any "error", or where an "alert" signals the need for same.

6) Further, every state provides for a recount when the total vote falls below a certain percent of difference between the candidates, impossible to conduct with the current EVM. And thus Congress must mandate the following regarding presidential candidates: A RUN-OFF election is mandated and triggered in those states where the percent of total vote is less than .5% of difference between the two candidates; said election to be held on the second Saturday following the election, on PAPER BALLOTS ONLY, and contain ONLY the names of the relevant candidates, for instance: "Barack Obama, Democrat" and "John McCain, Republican"— with oversight in counting by a representative(s) of each party—said procedure providing more than adequate time to meet the Electoral College mandate [Ideally, all of this could be eliminated if we did away with the Electoral College, but until then....]. NOTE: Had this been the law in 2000, Al Gore would be our president, and America would have been spared the economic, etc., disaster that followed!

7) Finally, absent the above safeguards, and until these safeguards are in place--Congress must mandate that PAPER BALLOTS, ONLY, can be used in our presidential elections. This is not a "partisan" issue, it is a "pro-democracy" issue. Most importantly, this will return the responsibility for our elections, and our vote counting, back into the hands of the individual voter, where it belongs, and out of the hands of "corporate control"---*it is after all "our democracy", itself, that is at*

risk if we don't take these steps---and in that regard, is there any time or cost differential that is too great?

Jim Green

CHAPTER FOURTEEN

I didn't write the following. It is a cut and paste from FACEBOOK, or some blog [would like to give credit if knew the author]--but it is so on target regarding how "fear" is driving Conservative policy in America today—i.e., is undermining America and our progress—and relegating America to a Third World country status, rather than a world leader—FDR had it on the nose in "All we have to fear, is fear itself"...at his inaugural in 1933....

"Conservatives are such cowards: they are afraid of gay people getting married or serving in the military; they are afraid of bringing terrorists to super max prisons in the US from which no one has ever escaped; they are afraid of the boy scouts letting gay kids in; they are afraid of everyone voting and are constantly suppressing the vote under some bogus voter fraud theory; they are afraid of letting students vote at their universities; they are afraid of women having the right to choose; they even are afraid of women getting contraception [the real issue actually is a women's agency and control over their bodies]; they are afraid of immigration reform leading to citizenship because they are afraid of-- name whatever reason; they are afraid of mandating gun purchasers to undergo background checks for crazy people and terrorists; they are afraid of people smoking pot; they are afraid of climate change being real and contradicting their beloved Bible; they are afraid of legitimate campaign reform; they are afraid of Muslims; they are afraid of blacks; they are afraid of atheists; they are afraid of hippies; they are afraid of socialists; they are probably still afraid of monsters under their beds; they are just rank cowards and keep making things up to be afraid of."

CHAPTER FIFTEEN

[I couldn't resist including this...and yes I am the author.....]

A MESSAGE FROM GOD

MANY CENTURIES AGO, a man of the cloth, we don't know his name, and in a flash of insight (perhaps induced by peyote) told his flock that "sex is a sin". And lo and behold he learned that by taking a very natural and healthy part of our life and turning it into something that was "dirty and nasty", that he could imprison his flock, and fill his coffers, and hallelujah it was a great day for the Lord!

Quickly, his miracle spread to other churches in his village, and then to the next village, and then the next county, and then state, and soon it spread to all the churches in the ancient world, and all of their flocks cowed in fear and shame and became imprisoned, and their coffers over-floweth. Hallelujah, it was a great day for the Lord!

And to keep the myth alive they started inventing stories, half-baked stories, that made no sense to anyone who is rational, such as "Mary was a virgin"— well, she just had to be a virgin because she would never partake in anything that was dirty and nasty, like sex (if you're doing it right), and this was necessary to make "sex is a sin" make sense...so they invented a Mary that was "sinless"--you get the picture. And their coffers over-floweth. Hallelujah, it was a great day for the Lord!

No one seemed to be bothered that when we play tricks on the human mind by taking something that is very natural and healthy, such as sex, and make it dirty and nasty that all kinds of bad things happen to the human mind:

Such as most pedophiles, and most serial killers, and voting Republican, and unwarranted suicides, and most mental illness, and unwanted pregnancies. (Teens not wanting to have sex is the perversion, not the other way around, and by replacing sex education and condoms, with unrealistic "abstinence", and by using blather about "low self-esteem" to shame them into not "sinning"—We have a teen pregnancy in the U.S. twice that of England and Canada!).

But none of this mattered, because their coffers over-floweth, and Hallelujah, it is a great day for the Lord!

There is a cure--------Tell our right-wing hypocrites, who Judge, rather than "Judge not".... to shove it....

GOD

ABOUT THE AUTHOR: I was employed in our Criminal Justice System for a cumulative 20 years as a probation officer, with 5 of those years as a chief probation officer. I authored the concept of "Shock Incarceration" which became law in Kansas in 1970, and then was adopted in numerous jurisdictions in the U.S. and also spread to Europe—it is currently identified in the U.S. as "Boot Camp" [as the means to "shock" the young offender—and a total distortion of my original intent—like many ideas, once released, they take on a life of their own]. I also instigated establishment of the first Court Psychiatric Clinic in the U.S., in conjunction with psychiatrists from the Menninger Foundation, as a chief probation officer. Finally, I was the Democrat candidate for Congress, District 21, TX, 2000. I would most define myself as a Social Ecologist-- [albeit my degree is in Psychology]. My web page is www.Inclusivism.org –which has been on the internet since 1996.
http://www.amazon.com/James-L.-Jim-Green/e/B001KHZIMM/ref=ntt_dp_epwbk_0

A BRIEF ADDENDUM: When the U.S. Supreme
Court denied certiorari—where the violation of my
constitutional rights were obvious, and criminal
negligence on the part of the government defendants in
the death of our son, equally obvious—[detailed in
THE HARVARD BOYS CLUB, Amazon/Kindle]--I
filed a Petition for Rehearing [which is automatic]—
and included the following. The Clerk of the U.S.
Supreme Court called me at my work in California,
and asked that I withdraw the "cartoon" [a reprint
from The NEW YORKER] from my Petition. I refused
on the basis of the First Amendment, and it remains in
the archives at the U.S. Supreme Court [Docket #: 79-
1627], to this day. The wording [not that clear] is:
"Excellent, excellent. A fine blend of truths, half-truths,
and blatant falsehoods".

IN THE

Supreme Court of the United States

October Term, 1979

No. 79-1627

JAMES L. GREEN,

Petitioner,

vs.

"Excellent, excellent. A fine blend of truths, half-truths, and blatant falsehoods."

OTHER BOOKS BY THIS AUTHOR ON AMAZON/KINDLE/BN:

- **THE HARVARD BOYS CLUB:** Hitler's Assault On Our Freedoms From His Grave

- **MY LETTERS TO PRESIDENT OBAMA:** Confessions Of A Compulsive Letter Writer

- **OUR GREED AND IGNORANCE:** Poses A Far Greater Threat To America, Than Terrorism

- **LETTERS ON STEROIDS:** Confessions Of A Compulsive Letter-To-The-Editor Writer

- **THE FIRST TIME I HAD SEX:** And, The Religious Intolerance Attack On America

- **WHY PRESIDENT OBAMA LOST THE 2012 ELECTION:** A Wake-Up Call

- **ECONOMIC INCLUSIVISM:** Neo-Capitalism/An Anthology: Inclusive pro-market solutions to our social problems

- **AMERICA IS ONE SICK MF:** Why Greed-Driven America Went Off The Rails....

- **EVERY GIVEN SUNDAY:** A Scientific Formula To Predict NFL Games

And others....http://www.amazon.com/James-L.-Jim-Green/e/B001KHZIMM/ref=ntt_dp_epwbk_0

www.ingramcontent.com/pod-product-compliance
Lightning Source LLC
Chambersburg PA
CBHW072114280526
45788CB00006B/2519